Beginner Sheet Music

For Alto Sax

Table of Contents

Table of Contents²

1. Ode to Joy (Anthem of Europe)

L. V Beethoven

Arrangement & Transcription by Willy Espinoza

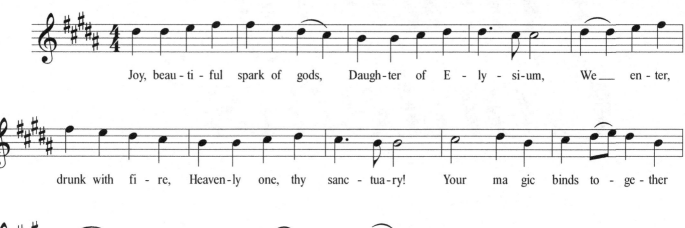

Joy, beau - ti - ful spark of gods, Daugh-ter of E - ly - si-um, We __ en - ter,

drunk with fi - re, Heaven-ly one, thy sanc - tua-ry! Your ma gic binds to - ge - ther

what __ Cus-tom strict-ly parted. All __ Men be - come Bro-thers, Where your gen-tle Wings a-bides.

2. Brother John (Frère Jacques)

Traditional French Song
Arrangement & Transcription by Willy Espinoza

Are   you   sleep - ing,   are   you   sleep - ing?   Bro - ther   John,   Bro - ther   John?

Mor - ning bells   are   ring - ing,   Mor - ning bells   are   ring - ing,   ding   ding   dong,   ding   ding   dong.

3. Happy Birthday

Hap - py birth - day to you, hap-py birth - day to you, hap-py birth - day, hap-py

birth - day hap - py birth - day to you.

4. This Land Is Your Land

Woody Guthrie
Arrangement & Transcription by Willy Espinoza

This land is your land   this land is   my land From Ca - li - for - nia   to the New York

Is-land From the red-wood   fo-rest to the Guff Stream   wa - ters   This land was made for you and   me.

5. I Saw Three Ships

The Chieftains

Arrangement & Transcription by Willy Espinoza

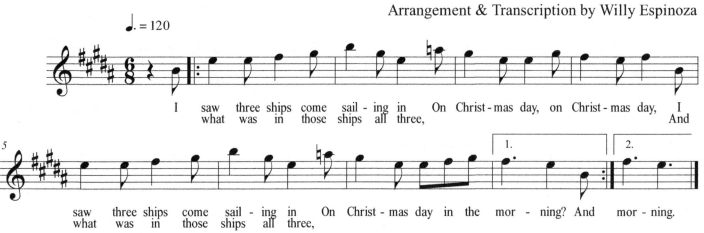

I saw three ships come sail - ing in On Christ - mas day, on Christ - mas day, I
what was in those ships all three,

saw three ships come sail - ing in On Christ - mas day in the mor - ning? And
what was in those ships all three,

And   mor - ning.

6. Auld Lang Syne

Doguie McLean

Arrangement & Transcription by Willy Espinoza

Should auld ac-quain-tance be for-got And ne - ver brought to mind? Should

auld ac-quain-tance be for-got And days of auld lang syne? For auld___ lang___

syne, me dear For auld lang syne We'll tak a cup o' kind-ness yet For days of ould lang syne.

7. Amazing Grace

John Newton

Arrangement & Transcription by Willy Espinoza

A - ma - zing grace How sweet the sound That saved a__ wretch like me
grace that taught my heart to fear And grace my fears re - lieved

I once was lost, but now I'm found Was blind, but now I see. 'Twas
How pre - cious did that grace ap - pear The hour I__ first be - lieved.

8. Aura Lee

W. W. Fosdick & George R. Poulton

Arrangement & Transcription by Willy Espinoza

When the black-bird in the Spring 'Neath the wil-low tree. Sat and rocked, I

heard him sing, Sing-ing Au-ra Lee! Au-ra Lee! Au-ra Lee! Maid with gol-den

hair. Sun-shine came a-long with thee And swal-lows in the air. Au-ra Lee!

Au-ra Lee! Maid with gol-den hair. Sun-shine came a-long with thee And Swal-lows in the air.

9. What Shall We Do with the Drunken Sailor

Traditional

Arrangement & Transcription by Willy Espinoza

What will we do   with a drun - ked   sai - lor?   What will we do   with a drunk - ed   sai - lor?

What will we do   with a drunk - ed   sai - lor   Ear - ly   in the mor - ning!   Way   hay   and up   she ri - ses

Way   hay   and up   she ri - ses   Way   hay   and up she ri - ses   Ear - ly   in   the mor - ning!

10. She'll Be Coming 'Round the Mountain

Traditional

Arrangement & Transcription by Willy Espinoza

11. Scotland The Brave

Traditional Scotland Song
Arrangement & Transcription by WIlly Espinoza

♩ = 120

Let I - ta-ly boast of her gay gild-ed wa - ter Her vines and her bo-wers and her

soft sun-ny skies Her sons drink-ing love for the eyes of her daugh-ters Where free-dom ex - pires a-mid

soft - ness and sighs Scot - land's blue moun-tains wild where hoa - ry cliffs are piled

Tower - ing in gran - deur are dea - rer tae me. Land of the mis - ty cloud , Land of the

temp - est loud___ Land of the Brave and proud, - land of the free.

11

12. Kum Ba Yah

Traditional
Arrangement & Transcription by Willy Espinoza

Kum-Ba Yah, My Lord. Kum-Ba Yah. Kum - Ba Yah, My Lord.
Crying___ Lord. Some-one's Crying___ Lord.

Kum-Ba Yah. Kum - Ba Yah, My Lord. Kum-Ba Yah. Oh,
Some-one's Crying___ Lord.

Lord!___ Kum - Ba Yah. Some - one's Yah.

13. Die Gedanken sind frei

Traditional

Arrangement & Transcription by Willy Espinoza

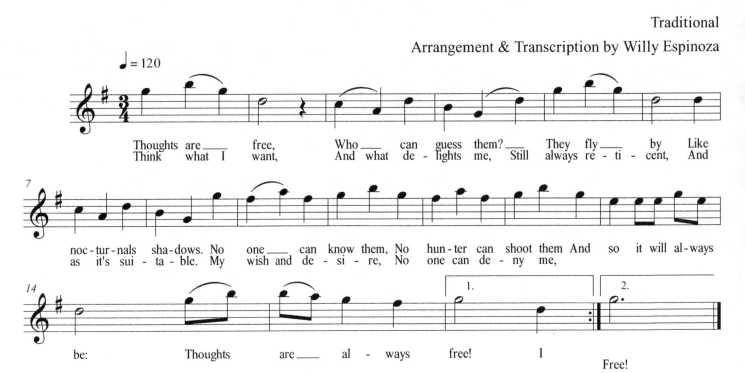

Thoughts are___ free, Who___ can guess them?___ They fly___ by Like
Think what I want, And what de - lights me, Still always re - ti - cent, And

noc - tur - nals sha - dows. No one___ can know them, No hun - ter can shoot them And so it will al - ways
as it's sui - ta - ble. My wish and de - si - re, No one can de - ny me,

1.

2.

be: Thoughts are___ al - ways free! I

Free!

14. America The Beautiful

Music by Samuel A. Ward.
Lyrics by Katharine Lee Bates
Arrangement & Transcription by Willy Espinoza

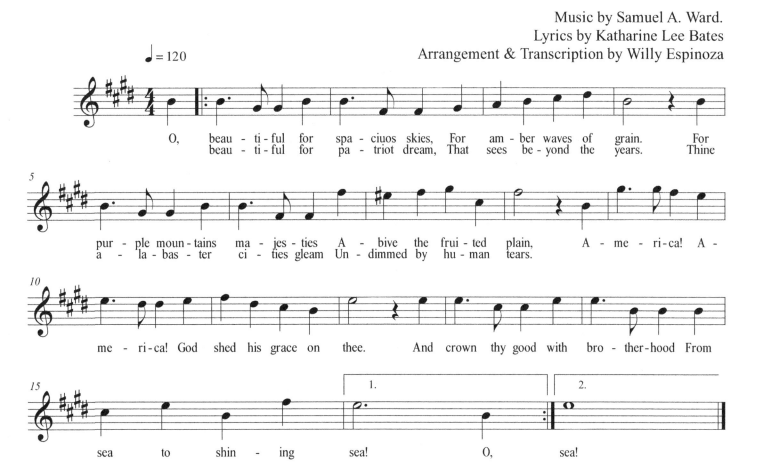

O, beau - ti - ful for spa - ciuos skies, For am - ber waves of grain. For
beau - ti - ful for pa - triot dream, That sees be - yond the years. Thine

pur - ple moun - tains ma - jes - ties A - bive the frui - ted plain, A - me - ri - ca! A -
a - la - bas - ter ci - ties gleam Un - dimmed by hu - man tears.

me - ri - ca! God shed his grace on thee. And crown thy good with bro - ther - hood From

1.
sea to shin - ing sea! O,

2.
sea!

14

15. Tumbalalaika

Traditional
Arrangement & Transcription by Willy Espinoza

A young la-dy's think-ing think-ing all night Would it be wrong, he ask, or may-be right,

Should he de-clare his love dare he choose, And would she a-ccept or will she re-fuse?

Tum-ba-la, tum-ba-la, tum-ba-la-lai-ka tum-ba-la, tum-ba-la, tum-ba-la-lai-ka, tum-ba-la-lai-ka

play Ba-la-lai-ka, tum-ba-la-lai-ka Tum-ba-la-lai.

16. My Bonnie Lies Over the Ocean

Traditional
Arrangement & Transcription by Willy Espinoza

My Bon - nie lies o - ver the o - cean, My Bon - ni lies o - ver the sea, My
Last night as I lay on my pil - low, last night as I lay on my bed; Last

Bon - nie lies o - ver the o - cean Oh, bring back my Bon - nie to me. Birng back,
night as I lay on my pil - low I dreamt thet my Bon - nie was dead.

bring back, Oh, bring back my Bon - nie to me, to me. Bring back, bring back, Oh, bring back my Bon-nie to me.

17. Oh, My Darling, Clementine

Percy Montrose

Arrangement & Transcription by Willy Espinoza

In a ca-vern, in a can-yon, Ex-ca - va-ting for a mine. Dwelt a mi - ner for-ty
Oh my dar - ling, oh my dar-ling, oh my dar-ling, Cle-men-tine! Thou art lost and gone for-

nin - er, And his daugh - ter Cle - men - tine Oh my tine.
e - ver Dread - ful sor - ry

18. Banks of the Ohio

Traditional

Arrangement & Transcription by Willy Espinoza

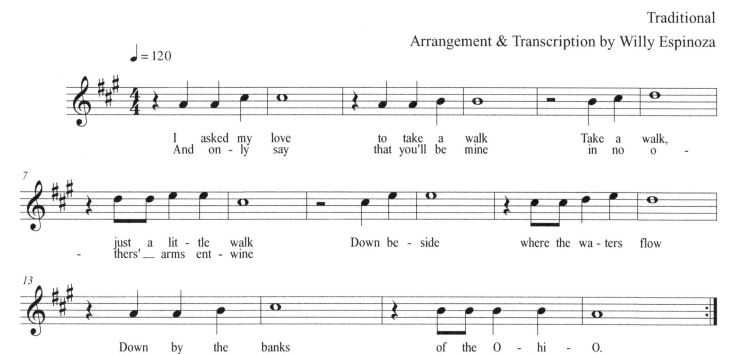

I asked my love to take a walk   Take a walk,
And on - ly say that you'll be mine   in no o -

just a lit - tle walk   Down be - side   where the wa - ters flow
- thers'___ arms ent - wine

Down by the banks   of the O - hi - O.

19. When the Saints Go Marching In

Traditional
Arrangement & Transcription by Willy Espinoza

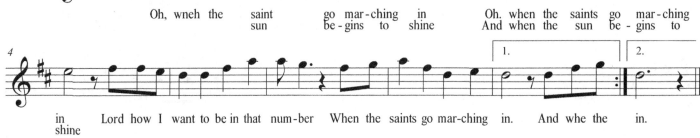

Oh, wneh the saint go mar-ching in   Oh. when the saints go mar-ching
sun be - gins to shine And when the sun be - gins to

in Lord how I want to be in that num-ber When the saints go mar-ching in. And whe the in.
shine

20. Wer ein Liebchen hat gefunden

Wolfgang Amadeus Mozart

Arrangement & Transcription by Willy Espinoza

Wer ein Lieb-che hat ge-fun-den, Die es treu____ und red-lich meint, Lohn' es
treu sich zu er-hal-ten, Schliess er Li-eb-chen sorg-lich ein; Denn die

ihr durch tau-send Küs-se Mach' ihr all____ das Le-ben süs-se Ser ighr Trös-ter, sei ihr
lo-sen Din-ger has-chen Je-den Schmet-ter-ling, und nas-chen Gar zu gern vom frem-den

Freund. Sei ihr Trö-ter sei ihr Freund. Sei ihr Freund. Tra-lal-le-ra, tra-lal-le-ra, Tra-lal-
Wein. Gar zu gern vom frem-den Wein. frem-den Wein.

1.

le-ra, tra-lal-le-ra! Doch sie

2.

ra!

21. Theme from the New World Symphony

Antonin Dvorak

Arrangement & Transcription by Willy Espinoza

22. For He's a Jolly Good Fellow

Traditional
Arrangement & Transcription by Willy Espinoza

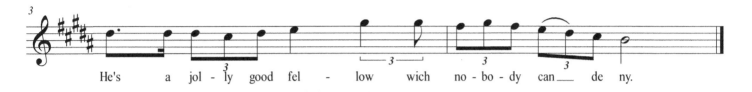

For He's a jol - ly good fel - low He's a jol - ly good fel - low for

He's a jol - ly good fel - low wich no - bo - dy can __ de - ny.

23. Spring

Antonio VIvaldi

Arrangement & Transcription by Willy Espinoza

23

23. Spring

24. 'O sole mio

Alfredo Mazzucchi & Eduardo di Capua
Arrangement & Transcription by Willy Espinoza

Che bel - la co - sa na jur - na - ta 'e so - le n'a - ria se -
Quan - no fa not - te e'so - le se ne scen - ne me ve - ne

re - na dop - p na tem - pes - ta pe ll'a - ria fres - ca pa - re giá na
qua - se 'na ma - lin - cu - ni - a Sot - to a fe - nes - ta to - ia res - ta -

fes - ta che bel - la co - sa na jur - na - ta 'e so - le Ma n'a - tu
rri - a quan - no fa not - te o' so - le se ne scen - ne

so - le cchiu' bel - lo, oi ne' 'O so - le mi - o sta nfron - te a

te _____ 'O so - le, 'O so - le, mi - o. sta nfron - te a

te sta nfron - te a te. sta nfron - te a te.

25. The Star-Spangled Banner

Francis Scott Key & John Stafford Smith

Arrangement & Transcription by Willy Espinoza

O__ say can you see, By the dawn's ear - ly light, What so proud - ly we
stripes and bright stars Through the pe - ri - luos fight, O'er the ram - parts we

hailed At the twi - lights's last gleam - ing Whose broad stream - ing And the rock - ets' red
watched, Were so gal - lan - ty

glare, The bombs burs - ting in air, Gave proof through the night That our flag was still there; O

say does the star-span-gled Ban - ner yet wave O'er the land of the free And the home of the brave?

26. Sleeping Beauty Waltz

Piotr Ilich Tchaikovsky

Arrangement & Transcription by Willy Espinoza

27. Wild Rover

Traditional
Arrangement & Transcription by Willy Espinoza

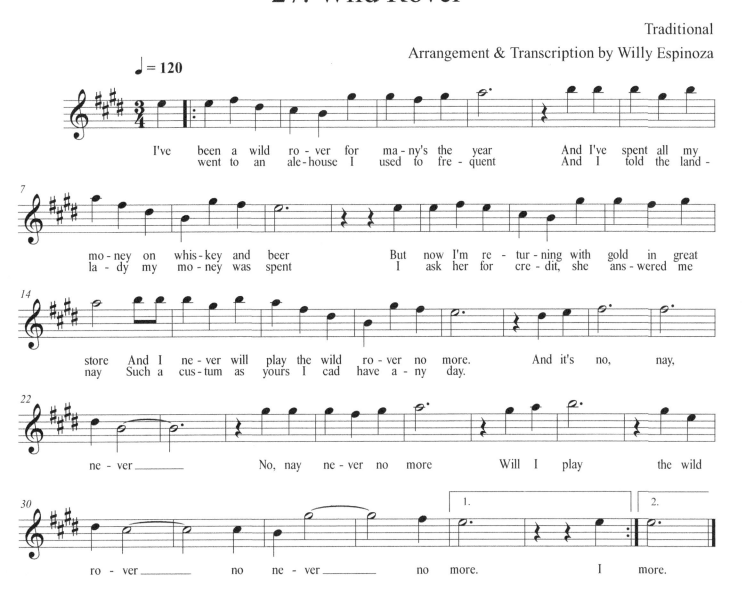

28. Can Can

Traditional
Arrangement & Transcription by Willy Espinoza

29. Oh, Susanna!

Stephen Foster
Arrangement & Transcription by Willy Espinoza

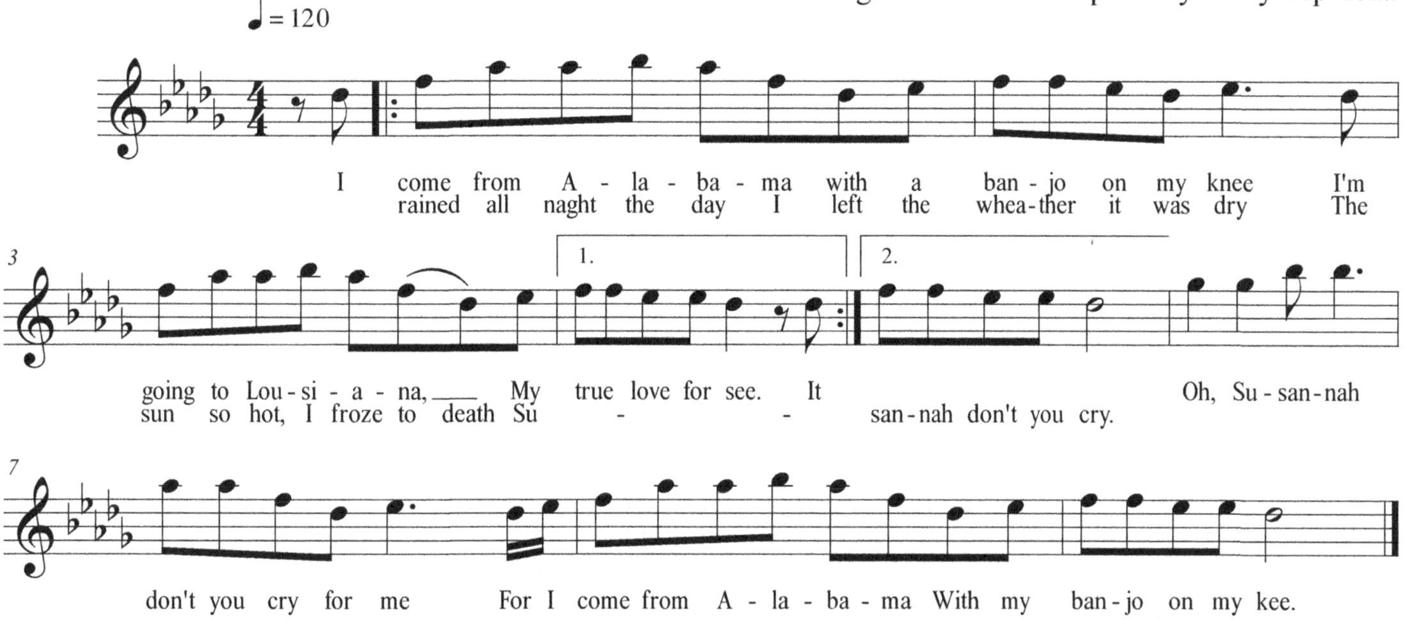

Lyrics (verse 1 / verse 2):

I come from A - la - ba - ma with a ban - jo on my knee I'm
rained all naght the day I left the whea-ther it was dry The

going to Lou-si - a - na,___ My true love for see. It
sun so hot, I froze to death Su - - - san-nah don't you cry.

Oh, Su - san-nah

don't you cry for me   For I come from A - la - ba - ma With my ban-jo on my kee.

30. La donna è mobile

Giuseppe Verdi
Arrangement & Transcription by Willy Espinoza

La don - na é mo - bi - le   Qual piu - ma al ven - to,   Mu - ta d'a accen - to
Sem - pre un a - ma - bi - le   Leg - gia - dor vi - so,   In pian - to in ri - so,

E di pen - sie - ro
é men - zong - ne - ro.   La don - na é mo - bile   Qual piu - ma al ven - to,   Mu - ta d'ac - cen -

to   E di pen - sier,   E di pen - sier,

E   E___ di___ pen - sier!

31. Greensleeves

Traditional
Arrangement & Transcription by Willy Espinoza

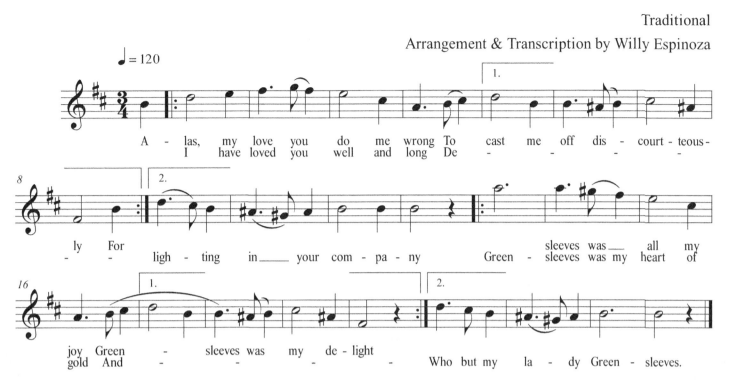

A - las, my love you do me wrong To cast me off dis - court - teous -
I have loved you well and long De - - - - -

ly For ligh - ting in your com - pa - ny Green - sleeves was all my
- - - - - - - - Green - sleeves was my heart of

joy Green - sleeves was my de - light Who but my la - dy Green - sleeves.
gold And - - - - - - -

32

32. Habanera (Carmen)

Georges Bizet

Arrangement & Transcription by Willy Espinoza

33. Minuet in G major

Wolfgang Amadeus Mozart

Arrangement & Transcription by Willy Espinoza

34. God Save The Queen

Arrangement & Transcription by Willy Espinoza

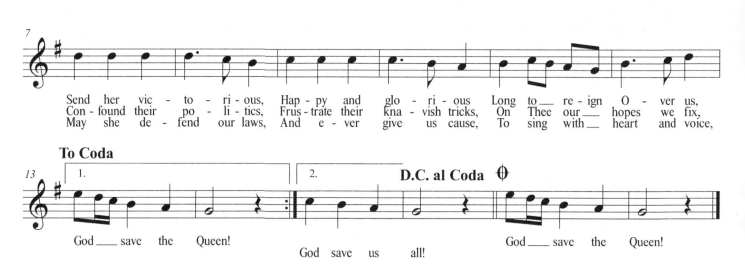

God save our gra-cious Queen, Long live our no-ble Queen, God save the Queen!
Oh, Lord our God a-rise, Scat-ter our e-ne-mies, And make them fall!
Thy choi-cest gifts in store, On her be pleased to pour, Long may she reign!

Send her vic-to-ri-ous, Hap-py and glo-ri-ous Long to__ re-ign O-ver us,
Con-found their po-li-tics, Frus-trate their kna-vish tricks, On Thee our__ hopes we fix,
May she de-fend our laws, And e-ver give us cause, To sing with__ heart and voice,

To Coda

1.
God __ save the Queen!

2. **D.C. al Coda**
God save us all!

God __ save the Queen!

35. The Oak and the Ash

Mat Williams

Arrangement & Transcription by Willy Espinoza

♩ = 120

A North Coun-try maid up to Lon - don has strayed, All hough with her na - ture it
fain would I be in the North Coun - try Where lands and las-ses are __

did not a - gree Wich made her re - pent, and do bit - ter - ly crey. I wish once a - gain for the
ma - king of hay, There shoul I see what is __ plea - sant to me, A mis - chief light on them __

North Coun - try Oh the oak and the ash and the bon-nie i-vy tree, They flou-rish at home in my
en - tic'd a - way!

own coun - try. Oh own coun - try.

36. Toreador Song (Carmen)

Georges Bizet
Arrangement & Transcription by Willy Espinoza

2

36. Toreador Song (Carmen)

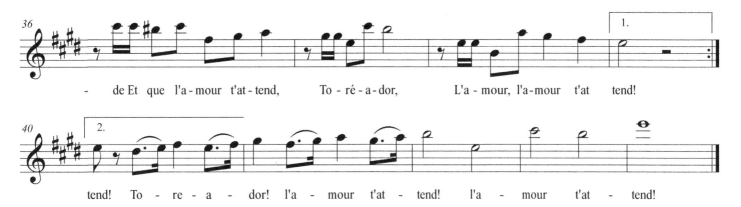

de Et que l'a-mour t'at-tend,   To - ré-a-dor,   L'a - mour, l'a-mour t'at   tend!

tend! To - re - a - dor! l'a - mour t'at - tend! l'a - mour t'at - tend!

37. Bella Ciao

Traditional
Arrangement & Transcription by Willy Espinoza

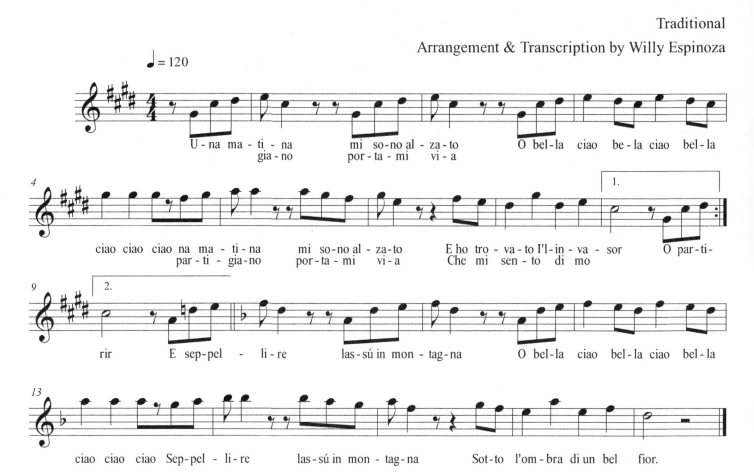

U - na ma - ti - na — mi so-no al - za - to — O bel-la ciao be - la ciao bel - la
gia - no — por - ta - mi vi - a

ciao ciao ciao na ma - ti - na — mi so-no al - za - to — E ho tro - va - to I'l-in - va - sor — O par - ti -
par - ti - gia - no — por - ta - mi vi - a — Che mi sen - to di mo

rir E sep-pel - li - re — las-sú in mon - tag-na — O bel-la ciao bel - la ciao bel - la

ciao ciao ciao Sep-pel - li - re — las-sú in mon - tag-na — Sot-to l'om-bra di un bel fior.

38. Tarantella Napoletana

Traditional
Arrangement & Transcription by Willy Espinoza

39. Minuet in D Minor

J.S. Bach

Arrangemet & Transcription by Willy Espinoza

41

40. Eine kleine Nachtmusik

Wolfgang Amadeus Mozart
Arrangement & Transcription by Willy Espinoza

41. Allegro in F major, K.1c

Wolfgang Amadeus Mozart

Arrangement & Transcription by Willy Espinoza

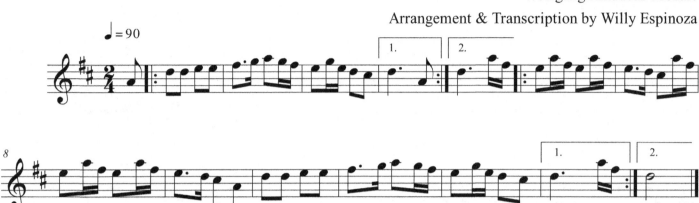

45

42. Swan Lake

Piotr Ilich Tchaikovsky

Arrangement & Transcription by Willy Espinoza

46

43. Wedding March

Felix Mendelssohn

Arrangement & Transcription by Willy Espinoza

44. Scarborough Fair

Simon & Garfunkel

Arrangement & Transcription by Willy Espinoza

♩ = 120

Are you going to _____ Scar - bo - rough Fair? Pars - ley, sage, rose -
Tell her to make a cam - bric _____ shirt
Tell her to find me an a - cre of land

ma - ry, and thyme _____ Re - mem - ber me to one who lives there She once
With - out no seams nor nee - dle work Then she'll
Be - tween the salt wa - ter and the sea strand Then she'll

was a true love of mine.
be a true love of mine.
be a true love of mine.

45. The Blue Danube

Johann Strauss

Arrangement & Transcription by Willy Espinoza

46. Für Elise

Ludwing Van Beethoven

Arrangement & Transcription by Willy Espinoza

47. Caprice No. 24.

Niccolò Paganini

Arrangement & Transcription by Willy Espinoza

48. The Entertainer

Scott Joplin

Arrangement & Transcription by Willy Espinoza

49. The Swan (Le Cygne)

Camille Saint-Saëns
Arrangement & Transcription by Willy Espinoza

50. March (The Nutcracker)

Piotr Ilich Tchaikovsky

Arrangement & Transcription by Willy Espinoza

51. Der Hölle Rache (The Magic Flute)

Wolfgang Amadeus Mozart

Arrangement & Transcription by Willy Espinoza

52. Symphony No. 40
(Great G minor symphony)

Wolfang Amadeus Mozart

Arrangement & Transcription by Willy Espinoza

52. Symphony No. 40

53. Turkish March (Turkish Rondo)

Arrangement & Transcription by Willy Espinoza

54. Hungarian Dance No. 5

Johannes Brahms

Arrangement & Transcription by Willy Espinoza

55. Adagio cantabile (Sonata Pathétique)

Ludwig van Beethoven

Arrangement & Transcription by Willy Espinoza

56. Hickory Dickory Dock

Traditional
Arrangement & Transcription by Willy Espinoza

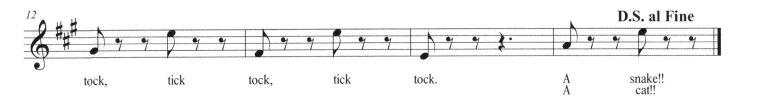

57. The Camptown Races

Traditional
Arrangement & Transcription by Willy Espinoza

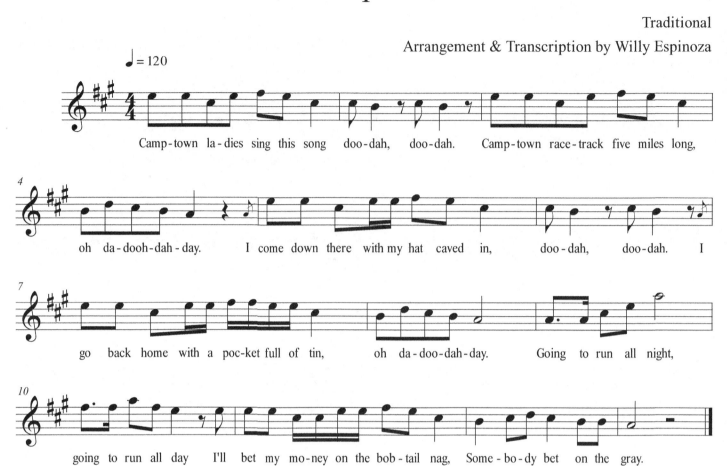

58. This Old Man

Traditional
Arrangement & Transcription by Willy Espinoza

♩ = 120

This old man,   he played one   He played knick - knack   on   my   thumb With a
                              two   on   my   shoe
                              three   on   my   knee

knick - knack   pat - ty - whack,   give a dog a - bone   This old man came   rol - ling home.

59. O Holy Night

Adolphe Adam
Arrangement & Transcription by Willy Espinoza

60. Five Little Monkeys

Traditional
Arrangement & Transcription by Willy Espinoza

Five lit-tle mon-keys jump-ing on the bed   One fell off and bum-ped his head   So

Ma-ma called the doc-tor and the   doc-tor said   "No more mon-keys   jump-ing in the bed"

25905155R00040